T0161204

NEVER SAY P*G

Never Say P*g

The Book of Sailors' Superstitions

R. Bruce Macdonald

HARBOUR PUBLISHING

HARBOUR PUBLISHING CO. LTD.
P.O. Box 219, Madeira Park, BC, VON 2HO
www.harbourpublishing.com

Edited by Martin Llewellyn
Text design by Libris Simas Ferraz / Onça Publishing
Printed and bound in Canada
Printed on 100% recycled paper

Harbour Publishing acknowledges the support of the Canada Council for
the Arts, the Government of Canada, and the Province of British Columbia
through the BC Arts Council.

Title: Never say p*g : the book of sailors' superstitions / R. Bruce Macdonald.
Other titles: Book of sailors' superstitions
Names: Macdonald, R. Bruce, 1962- author.
Description: Includes bibliographical references.
Identifiers: Canadiana (print) 20210394803 | Canadiana
    (ebook) 20210394854 | ISBN 9781550179798 (hardcover) |
    ISBN 9781550179804 (EPUB)
Subjects: LCSH: Sailors—Folklore. | LCSH: Seafaring life—Folklore. | LCSH:
    Sailing—Folklore. | LCSH: Superstition.
Classification: LCC GR910 .M33 2022 | DDC 390/.43875—dc23

Dedicated to Captain Richard Birchall,
STV *Pathfinder* 1978–83, who taught me
to *never* stir with a knife.

Table of Contents

Introduction

When I was a young man, I was hired on as part
of the crew of a tall ship. I came aboard with the
common land superstitions that I had never really
given much thought to, such as not walking under
a ladder, stepping on a crack, or letting a black cat
cross my path. I was soon introduced to the world of
nautical superstitions that would change my life.

Early on in the voyage I was preparing a cup of
tea with the most feared and revered person aboard—
the captain. We each poured a dollop of canned milk
into our steaming mugs. I picked up a knife and
went to stir mine when—in a trice—he clamped his
calloused fist around my wrist, with a grip that could
crush walnuts, and then leaned in to speak close to my
ear. With a voice that could be heard throughout the
ship he hollered, "Stir with a knife—trouble and strife.
Are you trying to jinx the whole voyage?" He stormed
out of the galley and I did my best to avoid him, as
well as all the disparaging looks I received from the
senior crew for the rest of the day.

Later that season, we were out in a storm where the wind increased daily, and the waves built to the size of houses. The gale tore out sails and we even lost one sail overboard. Day after day we tried beating our way into it making little or no progress. On the third morning, as the sun rose behind dark scudding clouds, a horrified cry came from up forward. Our figurehead—which carried the soul of the ship and something that we all felt kept us safe—had been ripped from the bow overnight. A jagged metal stump was all that remained.

The captain called all hands and we lined up in front of him trying to steady our weary bones by clapping onto the shrouds or pin rails. "There's a Jonah on this ship and I mean to find it!" he cried out and then stared at each of us. For a moment, each crew member wondered if his name would be called out, and then he would no doubt be thrown overboard with a "Jonah's lift." Instead, the captain left us standing on deck and went below. We could hear him rummaging around emptying lockers and duffle bags and then, in a booming voice, he announced, "Aha, I've got you now!" He climbed back on deck brandishing an umbrella, or what he would have called a brolly or a bumbershoot. Holding it above his head he cracked it over his knee and threw it to leeward. A smile came across his face. "We'll be fine now." A few hours later the wind shifted, the seas calmed and we began to make progress toward our destination. (Of course, we needn't have been worried about the captain. The crew's safety was of paramount importance to him.)

Since then, I've logged over 100,000 nautical miles under sail and had my own commands, including on that very ship where I nearly stirred the tea. Each vessel I have sailed in has had her own way of doing things; hence the expression "different ships, different long-splices," and each had her own superstitions. One thing is for sure: after all this time at sea I have never stirred my tea with a knife, and I have never taken an umbrella aboard.

There is evidence from the first records of people putting out to sea that superstitions have always been linked to sailors. Most of these are related to warding off bad luck. Before navigation became modernised and the world was mapped out in detail, sailors were literally sailing off into the unknown. In order to feel that they had some semblance of control over their collective fate, they watched for signs of danger, whether in the form of meteorological phenomena or the threat of witches, sea monsters or fairies, as well as the fear that Satan himself might be lurking somewhere aboard, waiting to snatch sailors away. Superstitions were the original marine insurance. As certain practices were tried and perceived to keep the ship and all aboard her safe, they were employed again on subsequent voyages and passed on to the next generation.

Landsmen might scoff at how ridiculous some of these practices are, yet perhaps when faced with a ladder in their path, might choose to walk around it rather than under it. Why tempt fate?

This book contains just some of the nautical superstitions that I have collected over the years. Admittedly, some are sexist, some are sinister and some are bizarre. In some instances, I have included the generally accepted beliefs that gave rise to the superstition. The reason that so many are still observed is because they work!

I encourage you to add your own superstitions or variations on the ones that I have recorded in this book. Write in the margins, highlight the ones that work for you and, like the sailors of yore, pass it along to the next generation of sailors. You can't be too careful.

Acknowledgements

Thank you to Robert Kondratowski of The Good Ship *Sylvester* for his encouragement to record all these superstitions. I hope that this small work answers some of your questions.

Thanks also to the Vancouver Maritime Museum for allowing me the use of their wonderful W.B. & M.H. Chung Library.

I am grateful to the Harbour Publishing team for their hard work and supportiveness, with particular recognition going to Anna Comfort O'Keeffe and Marisa Alps.

A hearty thanks to Martin Llewellyn for his copy editing, Libris Simas Ferraz for text design, Luke Inglis as editorial assistant, Coralie Worsley as publishing assistant, Amy Haagsma and Heidi Arnall. Thank you to my sister, Eleanor MacDonald of Queen's University for her helpful comments on the manuscript.

In the introduction to this book I wrote about a couple of experiences that I had aboard a sailing ship when I was a young man. This vessel is STV

Pathfinder and she and her sistership, TS *Playfair*, are now operated by Brigs Youth Sail Training out of Hamilton, Ontario (brigs.ca). A third vessel, *St. Lawrence II*, is operated by Kingston Brigantine Incorporated (tallshipexpeditions.com). I would highly recommend either of these programs to any teenager as a form of training that is, in my opinion, unsurpassed by any other.

I am much obliged and somewhat apologetic to my smart and beautiful daughters, Maida and Isabel, for their childhood patience in living daily aboard our ship with their "old man's" superstitious nature.

Finally, this book is in remembrance of my much-missed late wife, Sheila—forever my lucky star.

Adaro

A belief in the Adaro originated in the Solomon
Islands of a merman sea creature who absorbs the evil
part of a dead man's spirit. He is humanoid in shape
but has gills behind his ears, fins instead of feet, a
shark-like dorsal fin and a tusk protruding from his
forehead. He travels by sliding down rainbows or
inside waterspouts and attacks fishermen by throwing
flying fish at them in an attempt to kill them.

Albatross

Albatross are thought to carry the souls of dead
sailors and it is therefore considered unlucky to
kill one, although seeing one brings good luck. The
albatross superstition was made famous by Samuel
Taylor Coleridge's poem, from 1798, "The Rime of the
Ancyent Marinere."

And I had done a hellish thing,
And it would work 'em woe:
For all averred, I had killed the bird
That made the breeze to blow.
Ah wretch! said they, the bird to slay,
That made the breeze to blow!

Aran Sweater

The Aran sweater is named for the islands off the
west coast of Ireland. The patterns on the sweater
are unique to each family and they have been used to
identify the bodies of drowned fishermen (*see* Tattoos).
Knitted as part of each design are certain symbols to
bring good luck, such as the diamond stitch for wealth;
the cable stitch that looks like ropes, which is meant
to bring a fruitful day at sea, as is the lattice or basket
stitch, which signifies a full net; and the honeycomb
stitch for general luck. There is the possibility,
however, that this was all dreamed up as a marketing
scheme to sell sweaters.

Ash Tree

Some Irish emigrants fleeing the Potato Famine carved chips from an ash tree, standing outside a church in Cork, and took them aboard the ship as protection against drowning. In Norse myth, Mímameiðr is the world tree, a giant green ash tree that supports the universe, whose branches stretch out over the Nine Realms and whose roots reach into the underworld. Odin impaled himself with an ash spear that he then pierced into this tree and hung there for nine days to gain wisdom.

B

BACKSTAY

"Scratching a backstay" is said to give you a favourable wind. A sailor seeing a cat's paw ruffling the water's surface would stroke the backstay as one would pet a cat in order to bring forward more wind.

BAGS OF WIND

See also Wind Knots.

It was once common practice for sailors to purchase leather bags purported to contain favourable winds. If a ship was becalmed or faced with headwinds then the bag would be emptied to release an advantageous wind.[1] This is even mentioned in Homer's epic, *The Odyssey*, when Odysseus is given a leather bag by Aeolus, the king of the winds. "He gave me a sack,— flaying therefor a nine-year ox,—and in it bound the courses of the blustering winds; for the son of Kronos made him steward of the winds, to stay or rouse which one he would."[2]

BAIT

It is good luck to spit on bait before fishing.

Ballast

Rocks to be used as ballast are never taken from the sea because the sea will always be seeking their return and will sink the ship to reclaim them. In northern Scotland, since the late 1880s, a potential ballast stone that had been bored through by shellfish was always rejected as it had obviously previously been at the bottom of the sea. Ballast rocks that had been used in construction are never taken aboard either, as their association with the shore is too strong and they will seek to return.

Bananas

Bananas are so feared aboard some vessels that some sailors only refer to them as "that curved yellow fruit." There are three reasons for this. The first is that, since they spoil so quickly, they originally had to be transported to their market as quickly as possible, which meant that risks in high winds were taken, sometimes at the cost of losing both ship and crew. The area of wreckage would be littered with bananas that floated to the surface. This occurred primarily during the 1700s, in the trade between the Caribbean and Spain. Because fishing vessels were often used

for this trade and the bananas had to be delivered as a priority, it meant there was no time for fishing, which has made this fruit the most reviled aboard fishing boats. It is still thought that no fish will be caught while they are aboard.

Another theory is that bananas stowed in the depth of the hold would produce toxic ethylene fumes that might sicken or even kill the crew.

The third reason is that deadly spiders often hide in banana bunches or will have laid their eggs in the bananas that will subsequently hatch, leading to the crew being bitten and killed by poisonous spiders. Some captains will not even allow banana-scented sunscreen aboard as they believe the scent will scare fish away.

Banned Words

Words or phrases such as "drowned," "goodbye" and "good luck" are thought to be unlucky when said aboard or to sailors departing on a voyage. To reverse the curse, one must draw blood, usually by punching the speaker in the face.

Baptising

A child baptised with water from a rising tide will never drown. In the Canadian navy, a child of a ship's crew could be baptised using the ship's bell as a baptismal font. Often the child's name would then be engraved on the bell.

Basket

Losing a basket overboard was a portent that the boat would sink.

Basin

Leaving a basin turned upside down meant that the boat would overturn.[3]

Bathing

Before bathing in the sea, Swedish sailors would protect themselves from sea monsters by throwing in a knife, which would be retrieved as they went back ashore. In Scotland, bathers would throw in three white stones for the same reason.

Bees

Finding a bee aboard while at sea meant good luck was coming.[4] Bees were once seen as a link between the natural and the spiritual worlds.

Bells

If a ship's bell rang of its own accord, perhaps during a storm, it meant somebody aboard was going to die. If a church bell was heard from sea this also was a portent of death. When a ship sank, her bell might often be heard ringing as she sounded her own death knell. In the  age of sail, the ship's bell was much more than just a way to mark time; it was believed to carry the soul of the ship.[5]

On New Year's Eve it is considered good luck, at midnight, for the oldest crew member aboard to ring eight bells followed by the youngest member doing the same to ring in the new year. This is the only time that sixteen bells are rung, and as it caused such a ruckus it became unpopular to the extent that captains often ordered the bell clappers removed on that evening.

Sailors once believed that the sound of bells frightened away sea monsters.

Bible

Placing a Bible upside down on board will risk the boat and her crew. Quoting scripture except during a religious service is unlucky.[6] The most unlucky passage is Psalm 109: "Let his children be fatherless and his wife a widow." It was this "cursing poem," uttered by a sailor who had been unjustly condemned to death, that is said to have brought about a shipwreck near the Isles of Scilly, off Cornwall.

Birds

See also Seabirds.

If a woman saw a robin flying overhead on Valentine's Day, she would marry a sailor. If she saw a sparrow, she would marry a poor man but be happy, and if she saw a goldfinch, she would marry a rich man but her happiness would not be guaranteed.

Birth

Any child born on
a ship brings good
luck. The term "son
of a gun" refers
to male children
born on the gun
deck (the most
convenient and, in
many cases, the most

private place to give birth on a crowded ship). The
definition of a true sailor was that he "was begotten
in the galley and born under a gun with every hair a
rope-yarn, every tooth a marlinspike, every finger a
fish hook, and his blood good Stockholm tar."[7]

In Brittany, it was thought that boys would
always be born on a rising tide and girls on an
ebbing tide.[8]

Black Socks

See also Clergy.

Black socks are considered to be bad luck, particularly
on the east coast of Canada and in Ireland, since
priests wear them.[9]

Black Valise

Carrying a black case aboard was bad luck due to its similarities with a doctor's bag and was considered to be an omen of illness.[10] Conversely, "in the old British Navy, a seaman often made himself a hold-all from a piece of sail-cloth he then painted black; in it he would keep his most treasured possessions; the old expression 'to give a young lady his black bag,' was the sailor's way of proposing marriage to her."[11]

Black Walnut

It is bad luck to build a boat from this wood as it is also often used to make coffins.

Blasphemy

Taking the Lord's name in vain brought bad luck to the ship. Using euphemisms was common and was known as "cheating the devil"—hence, "cheese and crackers," "Jiminy Cricket," "Judas Priest," "gosh" and so on.

Blessing of the Fleet

Much like a christening ceremony, many boat owners participate in an annual blessing of their vessels by a religious leader at the start of each season, or prior to setting out on an extended voyage, to keep their ships safe at sea. Similarly, on Ascension Day each year, the Doge (Duke) of Venice symbolically married the sea by throwing a gold ring into it and chanting, "We wed thee, O Sea, in token of perpetual domination." This ceremony would ensure good luck for Venice for the coming year.

Blood

It is unlucky to set off at the start of the fishing season, or on a long voyage, without having first shed some blood in a fight or in an accident. Some sailors would seek out a fight on the night before a voyage for just this purpose.

BLUE

The colour blue on board was considered unlucky, particularly in Scotland and England, as it is traditionally the colour of a ship's mourning band. This was a horizontal stripe painted around the hull of a merchant ship on the death of the owner and kept for one year. Some sailors do not even allow blue paint on their homes ashore because of its association with death. Vessels would also hoist a blue flag or pennant to alert the authorities ashore that the captain or another officer had died and to allay any suspicions of mutiny. This is the origin of the expression "feeling blue."

BLUEBIRDS

Bluebirds are considered unlucky on the east coast of Canada and many fishermen will not even allow a picture of one in their homes ashore. The reverse is true in many other places, where they are considered good luck. They are also a popular nautical tattoo that represents hope.

Blue Cravat

Wearing a blue cravat aboard signifies death since it is the same colour as the mourning band of blue painted around a ship's hull.

Bluenose

A Bluenose or a bluenoser is a naval name for someone who has crossed the Arctic Circle. For good luck the person should have a quick dip in the Arctic Ocean or have ice cubes poured down their back. The ship's bullring or round metal fairlead mounted at the bow for leading towing hawsers or for making fast to a mooring buoy is painted blue in preparation for the ceremony. Not to be confused with the "Bluenoser," meaning a person from Nova Scotia.

Boat Delivery

It is bad luck to go and collect a new boat and to return without her if she is found to be unready.

Boots

Scottish fishermen who happened to haul in a left boot
with their trawl would spit on it and throw it back
in as the boot was a bad omen. If they caught a right
boot, however, this was a sign of good luck, and it
would be nailed to the mast to ensure good fishing and
fine weather.

Leaving boots or shoes upside down brings bad
luck. Putting boots or shoes on a table is forbidden as it
is a sign of death. Sea boots are never carried over the
shoulder when boarding a boat.

Bowls

A bowl turned upside down portends the vessel
turning turtle.

Brandy

Fishers in Normandy will stow a bottle of brandy
under the stern thwart since fish are supposed to be
drawn to its smell.

Bread

In many cultures, in order to find a drowned body, a loaf of bread was floated, sometimes with a candle in it and sometimes with quicksilver within it, in the belief that it would stop above where the body would be found. It was also thought that this brought comfort to the deceased. Others have used a cedar log or bowl for this purpose. A bun baked on Good Friday and stowed away aboard the ship will never go bad and will protect the vessel from fire.

Bread Upside Down

Turning a loaf of bread upside down once it has been cut brings bad luck as it means that a ship at sea will upset. This belief is most prevalent on the east coast of Canada. This may have originated from medieval France, when a baker would leave a loaf of bread turned upside down for the executioner, hence the overturned loaf became associated with death.

Brooms

While close-hauled and beating against a contrary
wind, the wind direction will change in your favour if
you throw a broom across the bows of an approaching
ship that is running free.[12] If becalmed, a wind can
be secured by hoisting a broom to the masthead with
the bristles pointing up to scratch some wind from the
sky. Pomeranian sailors would burn a broom with the
handle pointing in the direction that they wanted the
wind to come from or throw a broom handle overboard
in the direction of the desired wind. The luckiest
brooms to have aboard were those that had been used
to sweep inside a church. Hoisting the broom aloft
was also done in England when a boat's ownership
had changed hands, and in Russia it indicated that
there was a party or celebration taking place aboard.
In England, fishermen's wives would throw a broom
into the sea as their husbands set out for their boats.
Sometimes the broom would then be taken aboard for
good luck.

BROTHERS

There is an old tradition of not sailing with two brothers aboard. Three brothers meant even more bad luck.

BUCKET

Losing a bucket overboard is bad luck as it invites trickery from evil spirits. Buckets must always be stowed upright or a ship's luck would run out.[13]

C

CANDLE

In Romania, a candle must be snuffed out, as blowing
it out means that a sailor will drown. In other parts of
Europe, a cigarette must never be lit from a candle or a
sailor will die.

CANS

Cans must be stowed upright and must always be
opened right side up. Failure to do this brings bad luck.
This practice arose because it was believed that tin
cans might rust out at the base and leave food at the
bottom inedible. In opening a can the right side up, the
contents could be eaten more safely.

A similar belief is that everything must be stowed
right side up because to do otherwise was to invite the
boat to overturn. Retired fisherman Howard White
recalls that this superstition was religiously followed
on his ship, until on one trip out of Pender Harbour
on the west coast of Canada, Captain Jim Warnock
accidentally opened a can of condensed milk upside
down. That night his ship made a record set or great
catch of fish and he "thereafter insisted that milk
cans always be opened upside down." This is a great
example of the origin of a superstition.

CATS

Cats and ships have always gone together. They were welcomed aboard to keep the rodent population down because rats and mice not only carry diseases but can also get into the ship's food stores and cargo. There is evidence of Vikings having cats aboard in the 700s. Black cats were considered the luckiest aboard British and Irish ships; cats of all colours were allowed on board, however, because of their magical qualities. Some say that the belief that black cats are evil comes from a misinterpretation of the local language by British soldiers when they were in Ireland. When they asked what the cats were called they were told, "mi aorn" which in Irish Gaelic means, "my cat." They mistakenly heard it as, "mi adh," which means, "bad luck."

If the ship's cat approached a sailor, it was considered a good omen, but if the cat walked away from a sailor, then it portended bad luck. Some sailors believed that since cats were associated with witches, they stored magical powers in their tails and they could control the weather and even stir up a storm. When the ship's cat sneezed, rain was on the way. If a cat became frisky, there was wind coming, but if the cat groomed its fur against the grain, it would

be a hailstorm that was brewing. The wind would
come from the direction the cat was facing when it
washed its face.

Other superstitions include the following: while a
cat was rubbing its ear, the helmsman could not steer. If
it turned its back to the fire in the galley stove, the ship
would upset, and if it burned its claws, all those aboard
would drown. If the cat purred, then all was well.[14] If a
cat laid its forehead on the deck, then rain was coming:
"Cat on its brain, it's going to rain." If a cat was seen
climbing the rigging, then the ship would soon sink.

Some of these superstitions relating to predicting
the weather do have some validity, because cats have
sensitive inner ears and are, therefore, able to sense low

barometric pressure, which affects their behaviour. If a ship's cat fell, or was thrown overboard, it could create a storm, and whoever threw it overboard was cursed.

Some sailors' wives would keep a black cat at home as a good luck charm for their husband at sea. In Lunenburg, Nova Scotia, if someone did not want a ship with their loved one aboard to sail, they would keep their black cat under a basket, which would cause a delay in casting off.

In the 1590s, King James VI of Scotland (James I of England) was a fervent believer in witchcraft. When sailing back from Scandinavia with his bride, Anne of Denmark, they were caught in a terrible storm in the North Sea that he believed had been conjured by a witch. Under torture, an alleged witch named Agnes Sampson confessed that she had tied the male genitalia of a corpse to a cat and had then thrown the animal into the sea in order to sink the king's ship in the storm.

Some cats, particularly in the US Coast Guard, were so prized that they were issued their own passports, complete with photo and paw print. Manx cats are especially prized as, just like Manxmen, anything from the Isle of Man cannot drown and they would, therefore, keep the ship safe.

Caul

Having a caul, the membrane or amniotic sac that
sometimes covers the face and head of a newborn baby,
protected its owner from drowning.[15] This meant
that cauls were often purchased by sailors before a
voyage and advertisements for them were common
in newspapers. Captains liked to hire a crew member
that had been born with a caul, to ensure the ship's
safety. In addition, a baby born with a caul is believed
to have the power of second sight—the ability to see
into the future.

Children

Children on boats are seen as good luck as their
innocence keeps evil forces at bay.

CHRISTENING

See also Denaming / Renaming a Boat *and* Launching.

The ancient tradition of christening a ship can be traced back to the third century BC when the Babylonians would carry out a sacrifice to ensure a ship's safety. The Egyptians, Romans and Greeks also performed similar rituals: "An even earlier ceremony featured a priest, armed with a flaming torch in one hand and in the other an egg and some brimstone ... these two items would be offered to the deity whose image was carried aboard the vessel being launched."[16] Vikings sometimes used human sacrifice, a tradition that has evolved into the present day with the use of wine. Originally, red wine was most often used, to imitate blood. Missionary ships in the 1800s, by contrast, were often launched with milk. Eventually, champagne became the common choice, perceived as the most respectful and in keeping with the occasion. In England, it was once common for the skipper's wife to spread barley flour on the deck of a newly launched ship.

While the Greeks asked Poseidon to protect their vessels and the Romans called upon Neptune to do the same, modern ceremonies ask either God or some other sea deity to bless the ship and all who sail in her. It is considered inauspicious if the bottle of wine fails to break the first time it is swung against the hull; however, it is good luck to spill some wine or spirits on the deck.

Traditionally, ships were always named by men at these ceremonies, often a member of the royal family, but in 1811 the Prince Regent, who was later crowned King George V, began the tradition of having women perform the ceremony.

CHRISTMAS
To wash clothes on Christmas Day will cause a boat somewhere to sink. Putting fish scales under your Christmas dinner plates will bring good luck.[17]

CLAPPING
Clapping aboard a ship is thought to bring thunder.

CLERGY

Priests and ministers would typically perform
funerary rites, and so having one aboard suggested
their services would be needed. They were therefore
considered unlucky. They are also the enemy of the
devil; therefore, Satan would use the opportunity of
the priest being vulnerable at sea to
unleash bad weather. Even
naming their profession
was forbidden, and so the
clergy were referred
to as "the man in the
black coat" or the "sky-
pilot" and the church
was called "the bell-
house." If they were
named, clergy were
traditionally referred
to as chaplains aboard
the ship, in reference
to St. Martin,
who shared
his cloak
with a
beggar on

a stormy day. The cloak was preserved as a holy relic, which the king of France carried into battle. It was later kept at Sainte-Chapelle, in Paris, and the person charged with its safety was called the chaplain. The term "Holy Joe" (sometimes heard aboard to refer to a religious person) derives from Joseph Smith, founder of the Mormon faith.

In medieval times, priests were thought to be able to summon storms at will.[18] In Iceland it was believed that a priest who went out for a row would be taken by the sea if the church door was closed in his absence.[19]

Jonah, whom God punished with a great storm when he defied Him, described himself as a man of God—a priest by any other name.

COAL

A piece of coal found washed up ashore is a good luck token for a sailor. Pomeranian sailors believed that throwing a hot coal into the ocean induced stormy weather.[20] Aboard Arabian ships, in the 1400s, wind direction used to be predicted in a ritual during which the crew would gather around a table holding burning coals. One of the crew members would take a hot coal and swallow it. A rooster would be killed, and the crew member drank its blood to cool his throat before throwing the bird's body overboard. He would then be able to point in the direction from which the wind would come.[21]

Coins

Coins thrown into the sea as a boat leaves port means good luck (although pennies might cause a gale as such a small amount is insulting) and serves as paying a small toll to Neptune for a safe voyage.

Empty your pockets of change before fishing or your catch will be small. If a breeze is needed, have the youngest woman onboard take a nickel, spin three times, kiss it and throw the nickel into the water over her right shoulder in the direction from which the breeze was wanted.

Coins on Fishing Boats

Fishing crews cut a slit in the cork net floats and slip a coin into it to show Neptune that they are willing to pay for their catch.

COINS UNDER THE MAST

Placing a coin under the mast brings good luck. This tradition began with the ancient Romans, who placed a coin in the mouths of the dead, enabling them to pay the ferryman, Charon, to transport them across the River Styx to their afterlife. If a ship and her sailors were lost at sea, then the coins under the masts ensured that the crew's journey across the River Styx was paid for. The coins were traditionally placed "heads up" so as not to offend the sovereign but also as a reminder to the ship to head up close to the wind. On motor boats, the coin is often placed on or under the radar mast.

From ancient times, sailors perceived that the moon exerted some control over the seas. A silver coin representing the moon placed under the heel of the mast kept the ship and the moon in harmony.

COLD IRON

Touching metal and saying "cold iron" or simply
saying the phrase invoked protection from witches,
ghosts, and fairies.[22] It was generally used aboard
Irish and Scottish vessels if someone uttered a
forbidden word or took the Lord's name in vain. It was
also used as a substitute for forbidden words such as
"pig" or "rabbit." Because iron is a man-made metal it
is not controlled by supernatural beings, who rely on
manipulating natural phenomena. (It is for this reason
that graveyards are often fenced in with iron.) There
is a related superstition of touching wood, but the
power of iron is considered stronger; hence the saying
"Touch wood, no good. Touch iron, rely on."

COLLAR-TOUCHING

It is considered lucky to touch the collar of a
sailor's suit.[23]

CORAL

Carrying a piece of coral protects against hail and
lightning.

Cramp Rings

Once worn by sailors to ward off cramps should they find themselves overboard and too cramped up to swim, cramp rings were made up of braided rope or plant stems and worn around the thigh. Boys would sometimes be given eel skins to wear as stockings that were also called cramp rings. If they had been blessed by the sovereign, they were considered even more effective.[24] Cramp rings to be worn on fingers were made from screws or nails taken from coffins and protected the wearer from suffering a cramp while swimming and drowning. They were purchased ashore. These cramp rings are not to be confused with the cramp rings that were consecrated on Good Friday, to be handed out by the king, who had first rubbed the ring between his hands. These were intended not only to cure cramping but also to ward off epileptic seizures.

Crew Change

In England, it used to be a common practice for the skipper of a fishing boat to change his crew every season for good luck.

CROSS

Some sailors have traditionally worn crosses around their necks as a form of divine protection. Long ago, it was common for sailors to want to own a piece of the Holy Cross for that same reason. Con men ashore regularly took advantage of these sailors' desires. These bits of wood would be carried by the sailor or kept stowed in a safe place. Some Portuguese and Spanish ships had crosses on their sails to protect the ship.

CROSS-EYED

Meeting a cross-eyed person on your way to your boat was a bad omen, but speaking to them before they spoke would reverse the bad luck.

CROW

A crow flying across
a fishing boat's bow
means no fish will be
caught that day.

CUTTY SARK

Cutty Sark is the name
of a famous sailing ship
(after which a whisky is named) as well as a nautical
celebration of a witch. "Cutty sark" comes from the
poem "Tam O' Shanter," by Robert Burns. In the poem,
the witch Nannie Dee is depicted performing an erotic
dance wearing a small slip or undergarment called a
cutty sark. The watcher cried out, "Weel done, Cutty
Sark," which became a well-known saying in the
1700s in Scotland.[25]

D

DAVY JONES

Davy Jones is the most evil being on the Seven Seas. The name is most likely derived from the Devil Jonah or as a euphemism for Satan but may also derive from a notorious pirate in the 1600s named David Jones. Another possible origin of the name is the West African word "duffy" which means a ghost or devil. He is often seen standing in the rigging during storms or aboard ships as they are wrecked getting ready to lead the drowned sailors to his locker.

There is another story in which Davy Jones was actually a pub landlord in England, who used to drug men and put them in a box or locker to then sell them to ships as sailors.

DAVY JONES'S LOCKER

Davy Jones's Locker is the maritime version of Hell where wicked sailors go when they drown. A locker refers to a sea chest and Davy Jones collects not only dead sailors but also any wreckage from sunken ships.

DEATH ABOARD

The death of a sailor was a common occurrence
on long voyages. The dead body was placed in the
man's hammock that was also weighted with two
cannonballs, placed at his feet, which not only helped
to sink the corpse but also prevented the dead sailor
from following and haunting the ship. A coin, usually
a penny, was placed in his mouth to pay Charon to
cross the Styx. The sail-maker sewed thirteen stitches
to close the hammock and the last stitch pierced the
corpse's nose, not only to release his spirit but also to
confirm that he was dead. It was common practice for
the nose stitch to be performed by the dead man's best
friend. It was considered bad luck to keep a dead body
aboard, over and above the obvious problem of the
stench caused by a decomposing body. The body was
pushed over the side with a small ceremony. If there
was no ceremony, it was feared that the dead person's
spirit would haunt the ship. It is bad luck to speak of
the demise of a fellow crew member and use the word
"death." The adjective "poor" is inserted in front of the
deceased's name instead.

If the ship was near enough to shore that the body
could be taken ashore, then, in the interim, it had to
be stowed athwart-ships. Some crews held to the belief

that no one should go ashore until the dead body had been picked up by the undertaker, while others held to the belief that the entire crew had to disembark before the body was removed.

To have an empty coffin aboard was bad luck as it meant that one of the crew members would eventually be placed within it. Lord Nelson was famously given the gift of a coffin made from the mainmast of the French flagship *L'Orient*, which he kept in his cabin. It made so many of his crew uncomfortable that he had it stowed ashore and, later, it was where his own corpse was placed after the Battle of Trafalgar.

If a sailor was gravely ill, it was believed that he would only die on an ebb tide. This belief can be traced back to Aristotle, who wrote that "no animal expired except on an ebbing tide."[26] This may be the origin of the expression "when the tide is high, the end is nigh."

Debt

Sailors who had outstanding debts ashore were blamed for storms and for any other misfortunate events that would occur on the ship. A known debtor would not be welcomed as a crewmate. There is a common view that if one goes to sea and meets bad weather, someone has neglected to pay for his amusements ashore.

Other kinds of unlucky crewmates were murderers, thieves and braggarts.

Denaming / Renaming a Boat

It is considered bad luck to rename a boat, but if it must be done then there are some rules to follow. Legend has it that every boat has her name recorded by Poseidon or Neptune in the "Ledger of the Deep." By not following tradition and simply renaming a boat, the owner is being disrespectful to the sea god. The first rule is that the new name is never uttered aboard until the start of the renaming ceremony. The old name must be purged from the ledger and the god's memory. Before starting the ceremony, all traces of the boat's old name must be removed. This includes logbooks, equipment, books, charts with the vessel's name and of course the name boards themselves.

These things may be allowed back aboard after the christening ceremony has been completed. Nothing is allowed aboard with the boat's new name on at this time. The old name is written on a piece of paper and placed in a wooden or cardboard box, then the box is burned and the ashes scattered on an ebbing tide. A twenty-four-hour waiting period must be observed before the renaming ceremony. Beware of naming a vessel that tempts fate or shows any disrespect to the elements.

One additional superstition is that to ensure the new name is accepted, a sailboat must be sailed backwards (or by the sternboard) to erase the old name and a powerboat must be run aground three times. French sailors believed that August 15 was the only day that a ship could safely be renamed as it is the Feast Day of the Assumption of Mary to heaven.

DESTINATION

A sailor will never state their exact destination for fear of jinxing the voyage; instead they will say that they are heading toward a certain port. A ship's logbook should never be headed "To," but rather "Towards." Asking a sailor where they are heading will jinx them.

Dew

Dew on the deck at dawn is a sign that the morning
wind will be strong.

Dogwood

Thole pins made of dogwood keep witches away.[27]
"No boat left the Gabarus, Nova Scotia, boatyards
without dogwood thole pins."[28] Thole pins are vertical
posts set into a boat's gunwales that act as a fulcrum
for the oars.

Dolphin

Dolphins swimming alongside a ship are good luck.

Don't Look Back

Don't look back once your ship has left port as this can bring bad luck. Never watch a vessel or loved one go out of sight. This tradition most likely dates back to Genesis 19:17 when God warns Lot to "Look not behind thee," at the destruction of Sodom, although Lot's wife did not heed the warning and was turned into a pillar of salt.

Drake's Drum

Sir Francis Drake carried a drum aboard decorated with his coat of arms on his voyage of circumnavigation from 1577 to 1580. On his deathbed, he ordered that the drum be returned to England and that, if England were ever in danger, the drum should be played and he would return from heaven to protect his country. It has reportedly been heard several times sounding on its own, the last occurrence being at the start of World War I in 1914.

Dreams

A sailor dreaming of horses must prepare for high seas.

Drinking
The first splash of the
first drink goes overboard
for Neptune.

Drown
Saying the word "drown"
on a boat was believed to
beckon the possibility of it
happening.

Drowning
It was recorded in 1885 that
"Indians of Queen Charlotte's
Sound used a fetish of fish
bone to protect themselves from
drowning."[29]

EARRINGS

There are many reasons why sailors wear earrings including marking a circumnavigation, crossing an ocean or crossing the equator. Sailors have been wearing them since at least the reign of Elizabeth I. The superstition relates to the practice of burying the deceased with a coin in their mouth or two coins on their eyes to pay Charon to ferry them across the River Styx. A sailor who had drowned would be safe as he would always be able to pay Charon with his earring. For some, this also guaranteed a Christian burial if their body washed ashore as the value in their earring would pay for it.

Some wore them as a talisman that would protect them from drowning as it was believed Neptune would catch the drowning sailor through the earring with his trident, to lift the sailor back aboard. Still others felt that it improved eyesight in the eye opposite to the pierced lobe. For this reason, the captain would only pierce the lobe opposite to the eye used to raise the telescope to.[30]

Egg

Saying the word "egg" on an English ship brings
bad luck. This superstition arose in the early 1900s,
when eggs were only described as being "hen-fruit" or
"cackleberries."[31]

Eggshells

Eggshells had to
be broken into
tiny pieces to
prevent witches
from finding and
boarding the ship.
Witches would
board an eggshell
found drifting in
the sea and then
sail it back to the

boat from which it had been thrown overboard. Pliny
the Elder surmised that witches were known to prick
eggshells with the name and the image of the person
that they wanted to harm, which is why the shells had
to be crushed and broken.

Evil Eye

See also Figurehead.

The evil eye is painted on vessels, mainly in the
Mediterranean and Asia, and turns back any hexes
onto those who might try to curse the ship and sailors.
In Turkey it is known as a nazar.

Farewell

It is bad luck for a sailor's spouse to call out goodbye or good luck to them or to wave at them as they leave to go to sea. Goodbyes are said in private in another part of the home. "A goodbye from the wife is asking for strife."

Fata Morgana

A fata morgana is an optical illusion that makes ships appear to levitate and that was attributed to witches. The name derives from "Fairy Morgana," a reference to the figure of Morgan le Fay, a powerful sorceress and enemy of King Arthur (also his sister and mother of his child). In Welsh "mor-forwynn" means sea-nymph and "morgan" means mermaid, while in Greek mythology the three sisters of fate—Birth, Life, and Death—were known as the "Fata Moeragetes."

A fata morgana is caused when rays of light are bent as they pass through layers of air of markedly different temperatures (also known as a "thermal inversion," in which a layer of warmer air is above a cooler layer; an inversion of typical atmospheric conditions).

It is attributed to the "discovery" of ghost islands, ghost ships such as the *Flying Dutchman*, land masses, and even UFOs. It is most often observed in colder latitudes but was once reported on the Great Lakes, when the skyline of Toronto on the northern shore of Lake Ontario could clearly be seen floating in the sky from Buffalo at the eastern end of Lake Erie.

Feet

Flat-footed people were considered unlucky and were also avoided by sailors before they left on a voyage. The belief was that a flat-footed person would bring down bad luck on the ship, particularly as it was considered that they were more likely to fall from aloft.

Fiddler's Green

Fiddler's Green is located on the sea floor and is a heaven for sailors, populated by old shipmates, fiddlers and friendly women, whose songs can calm the seas; there is also an unlimited supply of food, beer and rum. The widespread belief was that to be welcomed into this sailors' heaven, a mariner must have spent at least fifty years at sea or have been a very valued crew member.

FIGUREHEAD

See also Evil Eye.

The figurehead evolved from the early Phoenician practice of painting or carving eyes on the bow of the ship. Figureheads were often carved to represent the person that the ship was named for or the qualities that her name evoked. They were believed to carry the spirit or the soul of the ship, and as long as they were watching out, the ship would be safe. The figurehead's eyes were carved and painted open so that it could see forward and guide the ship safely.

The tradition of a figurehead as a half-naked woman evolved from the belief that a woman's bare breasts calmed the seas. This may have derived from Pliny's *Natural History* in which it is claimed that a woman standing naked before the sea will calm it—"hailstorms, whirlwinds, and lightning are all dispelled by a faceoff with a naked woman." There is also a belief that when a sailor dies aboard, their soul joins the figurehead, to which they add their strength and wisdom. Others believe, however, that the soul enjoins the anchor. (*See also* Nudity.)

Fish

Chinese sailors will only eat a fish that is perched right way up. The backbone must be removed with the fish in this position or else their boat will be in danger of capsizing.

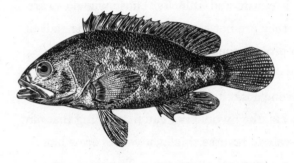

Fish Hook

If someone is caught by a fish hook, remove it and place the hook into a piece of wood, to speed the healing of the wound.

Fish Scales

It is considered good luck during herring season not to clean their scales from boots until the end of the trip.

FISHING

Empty your pockets of coins before going aboard or the catch will be small. Do not eat anything before the first fish is caught, and the first one caught each day must be spat upon and thrown back. Never count the fish until the day is over. Fishing every day of the week is considered unlucky. Those who do so are greedy as they are not satisfied with what the gods of the ocean provide for them.

Scottish, English and Swedish fishermen believed that if anyone spoke to them while they were heading to their boats, they would not catch anything that day. The only way to reverse this luck was to draw blood (perhaps in a physical altercation). To encourage a plentiful catch Scottish fishermen used to begin their fishing trip by throwing one of the crew members overboard, before hauling him back in.

FISHING NETS

When setting fishing nets, it is good luck to use an odd number and always to cast them to starboard, as that was the side that St. Peter fished from.

Fishing Rod

In Sweden, if a woman stepped over a fishing rod, no fish would be caught that day.[32]

Flag

Losing a flag is a bad omen, as is passing a flag through the rungs of a ladder. Sewing a torn flag on the quarterdeck is also unlucky.[33]

Flogging

French sailors had their own way of raising a breeze: by flogging the wretched cabin boy with his back turned in the direction from which the wind was required.[34]

Flowers

Because of their close association with funerals, flowers are considered bad luck and if, somehow, flowers are brought aboard they are thrown overboard before the boat is cast off.

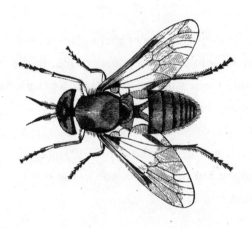

FLY
Sailors from Greenock, Scotland, considered it lucky if, when at sea, a fly fell into a glass from which someone was about to drink.

FRUITWOOD
As fruitwood was often used to build coffins it should be avoided when building a boat.

G

GARLIC

In Greece and Turkey bunches of garlic are secured
around a ship's rails to protect against storms. In the
medieval period, it was believed that garlic and onions
affected the lodestone—or compass—and were not
allowed aboard. According to biblical legend, when
Satan left the Garden of Eden he left the first garlic
plant in the imprint of his left foot and in the right
imprint, the first onion.

GHOSTS

Many sailors have reported seeing their drowned
comrades aboard, while others have been visited by a
spirit who helped them in some way. Joshua Slocum,
who completed the first solo circumnavigation, was
visited by the pilot from Christopher Columbus's
Santa Maria, who steered the *Spray* when Slocum fell
ill. This phenomenon is closely related to the "Third
man syndrome," in which other travellers have felt
the presence of, or even seen, someone's spirit who
provided companionship or aid.

Ghost Dog

In the 1800s a black dog on board a ship transiting the Welland Canal, between Lake Ontario and Lake Erie, fell overboard and was crushed to death. His ghost was heard howling aboard the ship at night for many years. He was also seen climbing aboard vessels that were heading into danger and then jumping overboard. He has reportedly also been seen on ships on both Lake Michigan and Lake Ontario.

Ghostly Sailor

The song "Ghostly Sailor," when sung aboard, will bring on a storm, as does the song "Young Charlotte."

Ghost Ship

Sighting a ghost ship spells doom. The most famous
of these ships, the *Flying Dutchman*, had a captain
who during his attempt to round Cape Horn swore at
God. When an angel then appeared, he fired a gun at it,
and was then condemned to sail around the world for
eternity. The oldest of the Great Lakes ghost ships is
Le Griffon, which vanished on Lake Michigan in 1679.
It was rumoured to have been cursed and has been
seen tracking a collision course with other vessels
on Lake Michigan, only to vanish just before contact.
Another ghost ship on the Great Lakes is the freighter
Bannockburn, which disappeared on Lake Superior in
1902 but has since been seen many times. Other Great
Lakes ghost ships include the *W.H. Gilcher* (Lake
Michigan), *The Western Reserve* (Lake Superior), *The
Erie Board of Trade* (Lake Huron) and *The Hudson*
(Lake Michigan). The two most famous ghost ships
on Canada's west coast are the *Valencia*, sighted off
Vancouver Island, and the SS *Melanope*, which was
hexed by a witch at the start of her maiden voyage,
had an unlucky career and was eventually scuttled at
Comox Harbour in BC.

GLASSES

Ringing bells at sea for any reason other than marking time, or for special occasions, foretold the death of someone aboard. This applies to anything that even sounds like a bell, including clinking glasses, which is why glasses should never actually touch for toasts aboard a ship. Running a wet finger around the rim of a glass to make a sound, is also forbidden because it echoes the cries of sailors drowning.

However, if the ringing sound is stopped quickly, then the devil would take two soldiers in lieu of a sailor. Stopping the ringing should be done with an uneven number of touches to the glass. Another association with any ringing sound is with funerals and, as such, foretells death.

Gordon Laco, who served in the Royal Canadian Navy, confirms that if perchance the rims of the glasses are clinked, then the base of the glasses should immediately also be clinked to negate the ringing and the bad luck.

British naval officers drink their toast to the king while seated, ever since Charles II, while dining aboard a ship, banged his head on the deckhead (bad luck for him) while rising for a toast. He decided that, thereafter, all toasts should be made while seated.

The traditional roster of toasts in the
Royal Navy are:

Monday—our ships at sea
Tuesday—our men
Wednesday—ourselves (for no one is likely to
  concern themselves with our welfare)
Thursday—a bloody war or a sickly season
Friday—a willing foe and searoom
Saturday—sweethearts and wives
  (may they never meet)
Sunday—absent friends

GOAT

At the start of a
voyage Scottish
sailors used to
hoist a goat's skin
(or sometimes
even a dead
ram) to the mast
head to induce a
fair wind.

Good Luck Charms

Sailors are notorious for carrying good luck charms or totems. Some of the more common ones are carved horns (England, Norway, Denmark); pieces of slate (US, Sweden, Scotland); small sugared skulls (Mexico); horse figurines (China); dried apples (England); animal and human ashes (Africa); wooden carvings of geese (Ireland); carved figurines of saints (France, Spain, Portugal, Italy); bat wings (Europe, US); bone fragments (US, Canada, Japan); otter skin (Shetland Islands); and the right front paw of a seal (Scotland).

Greasy Luck

While it is considered bad luck to wish a sailor good luck, whalers often wished each other greasy luck to encourage a successful hunt.

Green

Green has traditionally been frowned upon in the maritime world, mainly because it is considered a colour of the land and a green boat will want to run aground. Another possible origin of the unfavourable estimation of this colour is that some slave ships were painted green as camouflage, to hide in among the rushes near shore.

Hair

In Scotland, a man
would not put to sea
if a lock of his hair
failed to burn when
thrown into the fire.
If a woman burned
her hair while her
husband was at sea
he would drown.
Some sailors
carried a lock of their

wife's hair in a bag as a good luck talisman. A woman
combing her hair after sunset while her husband was
at sea would cause him to come to harm.

Harpy

A harpy is a vulture-like bird with long talons and the
head of a beautiful woman. During storms they swoop
aboard and carry off sailors with impure hearts away
and into the sky.

Harrison Lake

On Harrison Lake in British Columbia is "Doctor's Point where in the rockface stands the 'doctor,' naturally white-coated and red-hatted, who, legend claims, was shot by a vengeful Indian in 1880 and turned to stone. Everyone feeds the doctor by dropping crumbs into the lake," for good luck.[35]

Hats

A man wearing a woman's hat aboard will bring bad luck.[36] Leaving a hat on a bunk will bring death.

Hat Overboard

Losing a hat overboard was an omen that the trip would be a long one.

Hatch

Turning a hatch cover upside down is considered very bad luck, as is dropping a hatch cover into the hold.[37] It is thought that an upside-down hatch cover is an invitation for evil spirits to get below, perhaps because it resembles an open casket.

Hawseholes

These were originally carved and decorated as eyes, to allow the vessel to see if there were evil spirits ahead and to steer clear of them.

Holy Water

Some captains carried small bottles of holy water— water that had been blessed by a priest—to pour overboard in case of emergency.[38]

Horseshoe

A horseshoe nailed to the mast provided protection from storms. The horseshoe is always mounted with its legs up so that the luck does not run out and is secured with seven nails (a lucky number). The fact that horseshoes are made from iron also made it a good luck  talisman to touch. A horseshoe was usually nailed to a ship's mast and sailors sometimes carried a horseshoe in their seabag for the same purpose. Lord Nelson had a horseshoe mounted on HMS *Victory*'s foremast.

Hot Cross Bun

These cakes guard against shipwreck. Given to a sailor to take aboard or baked and eaten ashore to protect the household's family members at sea. Some sailors would keep them stowed in their gear to throw at storms to quiet the winds. The practice likely arose due to the religious connotation of the cross.

Inuit

In Inuit culture, a major taboo is combining seafood and the meat of land animals in one meal. This should always be avoided, because if the soul of your fish or seal or caribou tells the Sea Goddess about it, she will lay a curse on you.

Jenny Haniver

The name refers to a tradition that has been dated to 1558, whereby the carcass of a skate would be modified to look as though it had a human head. Once dried, it was sold and passed off as a preserved mermaid. The name "Jenny Haniver" derives from the Belgian city of Antwerp where these were often sold and where English sailors modified the French phrase "jeune d'Anvers" (meaning a young person from Antwerp).

Jonah

A "Jonah" is a person or object that brings bad luck aboard. The only way to restore good luck aboard is to remove the Jonah. The name comes from the biblical prophet, who, out of fear, defied God by sailing in the direction opposite to which he had been instructed. God then punished Jonah and all those aboard with him by conjuring a powerful storm. The crew threw Jonah overboard to appease God and to quell the waters, after which Jonah was swallowed by a whale. When he escaped from the whale, he made sure to follow God's wishes.

Klabautermann

A Klabautermann is a spirit that is found aboard ships
in the Baltic and North Sea and rescues sailors who
have fallen overboard. He is usually considered to be
a "happy" spirit, yet if a sailor saw him then the ship
was doomed to sink. On some vessels, a wooden statue
is made of him, typically dressed in yellow oil-skins
and a woollen cap, smoking a pipe and carrying a
caulking mallet. His name may derive from the word
"kalfatern," meaning to caulk.

Kelpie

A beautiful horse that lures the unwary onto its back
and then gallops into the sea. The rider lives below
the waves and cannot survive on land. Sometimes the
kelpie takes on the guise of a handsome man, with
seaweed in his hair, who lures women into the ocean's
depths. The kelpie may also sometimes appear as a
black horse with red eyes that emerges from the sea as
a warning of danger at sea.

KINGFISHER

A kingfisher landing aboard brings good luck. When becalmed, a dead kingfisher, when hung in the rigging, would always point its bill toward where the wind would blow.

KNIFE

See also Cold Iron.

If becalmed for a long time, a knife was stabbed into the (wooden) mast with the handle pointing in the direction of the desired wind. Rear Admiral D. Arnold-Forster recalls in his book *The Ways of the Navy*, "it is not unusual to see two rival ships' cutters drifting down between the columns of ships towards the finishing line, each with twelve clasp-knives stuck like hedgehogs' quills in their masts!"[39] This belief also relates to the protective properties of iron.

When giving a knife to a friend, a coin is always included to be "paid" back to the giver, or else the friendship would be severed. It was considered bad luck to sharpen a knife after sunset. A black-handled knife could be used by sailors to cut and slash at—and therefore weaken—the strength of the winds in a gale.

Saying the word "knife" was considered bad luck in the Orkney and Shetland Islands in the late 1800s; instead, "skunie" or "tullie" was substituted.

KRAKEN

These mythical creatures were reported to have a length of over 360 feet and would rise from the sea to pluck sailors from the deck with their tentacles. It is likely that they were in fact giant octopuses or squid.

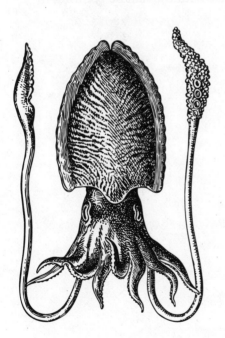

L

LADDER

A ladder carried aboard as cargo was considered to bring bad luck. This might relate to the land-based superstition of not walking under a ladder, because doing so breaks the Holy Trinity. A similar belief is that walking under a ladder invites the risk of hanging.

LADY'S TREE

The name for bunches of seaweed left to hang on the hearth to dry or in a vase to protect both the sailor's home while he was at sea as well as the sailor himself.

Launch Water

When a ship is first launched a small bottle of seawater is collected from near the bow. This is kept aboard as a good luck talisman.

Launching

If a ship turns naturally toward the sea when first being launched then she will be lucky.

Lawyer

Lawyers are known as "land sharks" to sailors and it is bad luck to see a lawyer when heading to the boat.

Letter "O"

Dr. Nathaniel Bowditch, author of *The New American Practical Navigator* and consultant to marine insurance underwriters in Boston, always refused to provide coverage for any vessel that had a name beginning with "O," as, in his experience, these ships were inherently unlucky.[40]

LEVIATHAN

Sea monsters have been witnessed and described by sailors for centuries. There are several notable examples recorded in the Bible. In Isaiah 27:1: "In that day, the Lord will punish with his sword—his fierce, great and powerful sword—Leviathan the gliding serpent, Leviathan the coiling serpent; he will slay the monster of the sea." In Psalms 104:25–26: "There is the sea, vast and spacious, teeming with creatures beyond number—living things both large and small. There the ships go to and fro, and Leviathan ..." In Psalms 74:12–13: "But God is my King from long ago; he brings salvation on the earth. It was you who split open the sea by your power; you broke the heads of the monsters in the waters." And, finally, in Job 41:1–2, 7–10, 13–34:

> *Can you pull in the Leviathan with a fishhook or tie down his tongue with a rope? Can you put a cord through his nose or pierce his jaw with a hook?*
>
> *Can you fill his hide with harpoons or his head with fishing spears? If you lay a hand on him, you will remember the struggle and never do it again! Any hope of subduing him*

is false; the mere sight of him is overpowering.
No one is fierce enough to rouse him. Who
then is able to stand against me?

Who can strip off its outer coat? Who can
penetrate its double coat of armor? Who dares
open the doors of its mouth, ringed about with
fearsome teeth? Its back has rows of shields
tightly sealed together; each is so close to the
next that no air can pass between. They are
joined fast to one another; they cling together
and cannot be parted. Its snorting throws out
flashes of light; its eyes are like the rays of
dawn. Flames stream from its mouth; sparks
of fire shoot out. Smoke pours from its nostrils

as from a boiling pot over burning reeds. Its
breath sets coals ablaze, and flames dart
from its mouth. Strength resides in its neck;
dismay goes before it. The folds of its flesh are
tightly joined; they are firm and immovable.
Its chest is hard as rock, hard as a lower
millstone. When it rises up, the mighty are
terrified; they retreat before its thrashing. The
sword that reaches it has no effect, nor does
the spear or the dart or the javelin. Iron it
treats like straw and bronze like rotten wood.
Arrows do not make it flee; slingstones are
like chaff to it. A club seems to it but a piece
of straw; it laughs at the rattling of the lance.
Its undersides are jagged potsherds, leaving
a trail in the mud like a threshing sledge. It
makes the depths churn like a boiling caldron
and stirs up the sea like a pot of ointment. It
leaves a glistening wake behind it; one would
think the deep had white hair. Nothing on
earth is its equal—a creature without fear. It
looks down on all that are haughty; it is king
over all that are proud.

LIGHTS

Leaving three lights burning on a table in a room ashore means that a ship at sea will overturn.

LINE CROSSING

The line crossing ceremony is held for a sailor crossing the equator for the first time. Until the crossing, they are known as pollywogs, but after the ceremony, they are referred to as Shellbacks or the Son (or Daughter) of Neptune. The ceremony usually involves a visit from King Neptune and some friends who put the pollywogs through several trials to prove their worthiness of the honoured title. These days the equator ceremony is generally the only one that is still observed but it was once common to hold similar ceremonies when passing other significant points of land or different latitudes, entering different oceans or lakes and so on.

Manta Rays

Manta rays, also known as devilfish or sea devils, were feared as much as sharks, as sailors believed they could attach themselves to a ship's anchor and drag her under the waves to Davy Jones's Locker.

Mermaids and Mermen

Sighting a mermaid or merman is generally an unlucky event. Some believed that they could grant a wish or confer wealth but most tales revolve around them telling sailors they were

86

doomed. Sighting a mer-creature could also have been a sign that a bad storm was heading for the ship. However, Manxmen were considered to be descended from mermen and therefore were unable to drown. For that reason, they were always welcome aboard as crew members.

MICHIGAN MITTEN

Great Lakes sailors were once fearful of sailing on an inverted U-shaped voyage, something that happens when a trip is planned around a peninsula. This mitten shape occurs, for instance, on a route from Toledo, Ohio, to Chicago, or between Detroit and Milwaukee. The reason behind this may have been that the inverted U resembles an upside-down horseshoe, which is a very unlucky symbol.

MISHIBIJIW / MISHIPESHU

In Ojibwa myth, Mishibijiw is the name of the dragon of Lake Superior. It has the body of a lynx, scales, horns growing from its head, rigid spines down its back and webbed paws.

MITTENS

In Lunenburg, on the east coast of Canada, it is
bad luck to wear white mittens on board, and, ten
miles away in Mahone Bay, it is bad luck to wear
grey mittens at sea. Grey mittens are bad luck
since undertakers traditionally wore grey mittens.[41]
Whatever the colour, it is extremely bad luck to have a
coloured ring knit into the cuff of a mitten.

MOON

When the moon appears with its horns pointing up as
though it could contain water it is a sign that it will
rain: "The moon on her back holds water in her lap." A
halo around the moon indicates that rain is coming.

Moonlight

A common rhyme once taught to children who saw
the moon shining into their rooms was "I see the
moon and the moon sees me, God bless the sailors
on the sea."

Moon Line

When the moon casts a glow across the deck a sailor
will not step into this space of light for fear of bad
luck. This fear of the moon is where we get the terms
lunatic and *lunacy*.

Mop

Losing a mop overboard is unlucky, as is hanging a
mop overboard.

Mugs

If a mug is stowed on a hook, then the handle should
always face forward with the rim facing aft. This is a
practice for good luck but may have originated from
a time when mugs would have been stowed out in an
open cockpit and, if they were not hung in this way,
would have filled with seawater.

Nails

See also Personal Grooming.

In Norse mythology is *Naglfar*, a ship constructed of the clipped fingernails of sailors and full of the world's chaos that will be used in a battle between the gods. The ship is said to be unfinished and any sailor drowning who has long nails will provide the missing parts needed and then chaos would be unleashed. A variation on this legend is also found in Icelandic culture, where sailors would have to cut their trimmed nails into pieces or else Satan would use them to construct his own ship.

Narwhal

Sailors from Greenland believed that narwhals were the reincarnation of lost sailors. Icelandic sailors held that a narwhal would swim in front of a ship that was doomed to sink. Narwhal tusks were often represented as unicorn horns and were considered very good luck to have aboard. Even when the horn was known to be from a narwhal, it was still considered to be good luck because of the association with the unicorn.

NON-SAILING DAYS

There are many "dies infausti" or unlucky days to avoid when setting out to sea. The most famous day not to start a voyage on is a Friday. This brought about the expression "Friday sail, always fail." This could arise from the belief that Friday was the day that Jesus was crucified; it also could refer to Norse myth, in which Friday was traditionally the day witches would hold their coven. Friday was named for the Norse deity Frigga, the goddess of love and fertility, but whom Christians thought to be a witch.

The superstition of Friday being an unlucky day did not arise, however, until five centuries after the Crucifixion. Thus, the association of Friday with bad luck may also have resulted from the arrest of the Grand Master of the Knights Templar, Jacques de Molay on Friday, October 13, 1307. His arrest marked the fall of the Order. Ending a voyage on a Friday only postponed bad luck until the next sailing date. Conversely, Spanish sailors thought Friday to be a lucky day to begin a voyage as this was the day Columbus had set sail in 1492.

Thursdays are also unlucky days since Thursday is named after Thor, the god of storms and thunder.

Candlemas (in early February) is also considered unlucky, as is the first Monday in April, which was supposedly the day on which Cain killed Abel. The second Monday in August was supposedly the day Sodom and Gomorrah were destroyed, and December 31, the day on which Judas Iscariot hanged himself, is also unlucky. The seventeenth and twenty-ninth of any month were considered the luckiest for setting out on a long voyage and Sundays were generally favourable for casting off, as the Resurrection of Jesus was on a Sunday.

Noose

It is bad luck to tie a noose on a ship, as it invites death aboard. If one is needed, then it should always be made with thirteen counter-clockwise turns (or "widdershins," meaning to walk around something on the left; unlucky because it was contrary to the direction of the sun). The thirteen turns invited Davy Jones (the devil) to take the condemned to his locker.[42] On a practical note, thirteen turns makes for a very bulky and unwieldy noose.

North Star

See also Tattoos.

The North Star, or Polaris, is known as the navigator's star since it will always guide a sailor. To this end, a star is often mounted on the head of the bowsprit and the booms.[43]

Nudity

In Catalonia, it was common practice for fishermen's wives to expose their genitals to the sea to calm it before their husbands set out. "La mer es posa bona si veu el cony d'una dona" was the common expression ("The sea calms down if it sees a woman's vagina").

O

Oak

Oak is thought to possess magical qualities, and in traditional shipbuilding, the keel should be aligned in a north-south direction and kept out of sight of women.

Oil

Oil on rough seas helps to temporarily keep waves from breaking. A few token drops cast to windward are also thought to help calm the seas. There is some practical truth to this as the oil does temporarily break the surface tension, particularly when significant quantities are released.

Orca

The orca, or killer whale, was "regarded in Christian folklore as a symbol of the devil, the sea creature thought able to lure fish into its maw by wafting its sweet breath over its prey ... it was believed that the devil lured folk into sin by the same means."[44]

Oyster Dredging

Oyster fishers are known for making a drone-like sound to "charm the oysters into their net." Some of the traditional lyrics are: "The herring loves the merry moonlight / The mackerel loves the wind / But the oyster loves the dredger's song / For he comes of gentle kind."

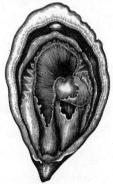

Painter

If a knot is found in the painter—the line that is
attached to a small boat and is used for tying up or
towing—before casting off, it will be an unhappy
voyage. This is because it is a witch's knot and,
therefore, a hex has been put on the boat.

Patron Saints & Deities

There are many saints to whom sailors have prayed.
St. Nicolas was often called upon since he is said to
have calmed a storm through prayer. The English
nicknamed Portuguese and Spanish sailors "dagos,"
a mishearing of "Diego," to whom the latter often
prayed as their patron saint. In Portugal, Italy, France
and Spain, St. Anthony is the patron saint of sailors
and fishermen. His statue was sometimes placed in a
shrine on the ship's mast. He is also the patron saint of
the wind, and so, when the wind died, it was thought
he was asleep and sailors would whistle to him or
swear at him to rouse him.

St. Brendan the Navigator is also prayed to for
obvious reasons. St. Erasmus, also known as St. Elmo,
is famous for having declared—before dying at sea in
a storm—that he would reveal himself to let sailors

know that they would be safe. A glowing light was then seen at the masthead, proving that he had kept his word. Since then, the electrical discharge that causes yards and masts to glow is called St. Elmo's Fire. If, however, this phenomenon appears around a sailor's head, then he will die within a day.

St. Clement is also known as the sailor's saint, and his symbol is a stylised cross and anchor, as he was drowned with an anchor around his neck as punishment for converting many to his faith. He is also the guardian against gales and storms.

St. Christina is the female patron saint of mariners. St. Patrick banished pagan women from the land by turning them into mermaids. Mami Wata ("Mother Water") was a goddess worshipped mainly in Africa and parts of the Caribbean; her upper body is in human form and her lower body resembles a fish or a snake.

In Brazil and Cuba, sailors worshipped the sea goddess Yemaya, who protects boats and delivers fish to fishermen. In Hong Kong and China, the sea goddess is known as Tin Hau, also known as Mazu, who protects boats and those aboard them.

PERIDOT
The wearing of an eagle-shaped charm made from the gemstone peridot gives the wearer control over the wind and wards off evil forces.

Personal Grooming

It is bad luck to cut your nails or trim your hair or shave your beard aboard, as the clippings and locks might be considered an offering to Proserpina, the goddess of the underworld. This could provoke Neptune's jealousy because offerings were being made to someone other than him. A related belief is that once Neptune gets a taste of you, he might reach up to have some more.

Pig

The word "pig" is unlucky and so is never said aboard and is substituted with "curly-tail," "Mr. Dennis," "little fella" or "gruff." Sometimes they are called a "cauldie," which was a slang word for "cold iron." Seeing a pig while travelling to your boat is a sign of impending danger and has caused many a sailor and fisherman to turn back and go home to await another day to set sail. If the word "pig" is uttered it will cause a storm since it is thought that pigs can see the wind.

This belief probably stems from the Gospel of Matthew 8:28–34, when two men were possessed by demons. Upon seeing Jesus and believing that they were damned, they begged Jesus to drive the demons out and into a herd of swine on a far cliff. Jesus did this and the pigs ran over the cliff and drowned in the Sea of Galilee.

Killing a pig aboard a ship will bring about terrible weather called a pig-storm and eating pork aboard is also sure to cause misfortune. Another unlucky association is with the devil, because pigs also have cloven hooves. The five dark marks often found on the inside of a pig's trotter are the marks of the devil's claw.

Pineapple

The pineapple is a symbol of good luck and prosperity at sea. When the ship was back in port and safely unloaded, a captain might return home with a pineapple in hand. He would spear this fruit onto the front gate to show friends and neighbours that he had safely returned.

Pins

Pins are considered unlucky to have aboard as they serve no practical purpose and were once considered witches' instruments.

Plants

Plants or trees
should not be
aboard since they
will seek to be on
dry ground and
cause the ship to
run aground.

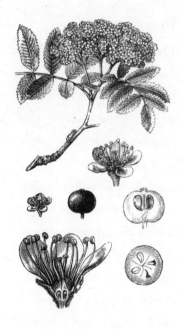

Playing Cards

Playing cards were once considered unlucky to have
aboard a ship, and they were known as the "devil's
picture-book." But tearing up a deck of cards and
casting them overboard would bring good luck.

Pointing

Pointing with one finger is considered bad luck,
particularly if the offending digit is aimed toward a
boat. One must use the entire hand to indicate what
one is trying to draw attention to.

Pom-pom

In France, touching the red pom-pom on a sailor's hat
will bring you good luck. They were supposed to have
originally been sewn on as protection against sailors
banging their heads on the low deckheads.

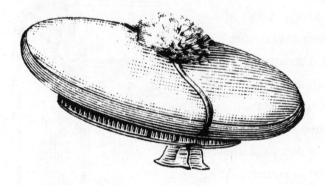

POURING FROM A BOTTLE

Italian sailors, as well as those from other European countries, consider it unlucky to pour wine with the left hand "like a traitor," because apparently Judas did so. Some interpreted this as a sign that the person whose glass was being filled was being revealed as a traitor.

Pouring wine or other spirits underhanded—that is, with one's palm facing up and the back of the hand toward the glass— was also considered very unlucky for the person whose glass was being filled. This most likely derived from the supposed practice of assassins who wore rings containing poison and who would, therefore, position their hand in such a way as to allow the poison to pour into the glass unnoticed. Pouring this way was therefore taken as a sign, to the person whose glass was being filled and those around the table, that you wished death on them.

Prostitute

It was a common belief in England in the 1600s that having a prostitute aboard would cause a storm.

Puck

French sailors sometimes complained of being visited during their night watches by the spirit "Puck," who played pranks on them such as opening the knives in their pockets, undoing the furled sails or singeing their hair. The name Puck comes from the older name "pouque," meaning "devil" or "evil spirit."

Q

QALUPALIK

The Qalupalik is a creature of Inuit legend described as human-like but with green skin, long hair and very long fingernails. She lives in the sea and hums to entice children to come closer to the water where she will drag them in.

Rabbit

Rabbits are referred to as long, floppy-eared animals with fluffy tails or sometimes "ground pheasants" aboard ships, as even saying "rabbit" is unlucky. This superstition originally derived from the belief that the devil could disguise himself as a rabbit. Later, this also included witches gaining the ability to turn themselves into rabbits. The practice of carrying a rabbit's foot was to show the devil or a witch that you were capable of killing rabbits and therefore should not be trifled with. Having a dead rabbit aboard was considered very bad luck and no skipper would sail the same day it had been found. One children's prank was to hide a dead rabbit aboard a fishing boat and then watch as the crew got angry or scared once it was found.

Rainbow

Pointing at a rainbow brings bad luck or, at the very least, rain. To draw attention to it, you must describe its location.

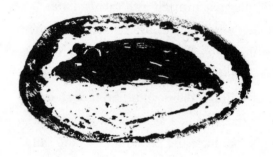

Rats

It is considered bad luck to call them by name, and so aboard ships they are referred to as "long-tails." In the Royal Navy they were known as "millers" as their coats were often dusted with flour from breaking into the ship's stores. If rats left a ship just before she sailed, the ship was doomed. This was because they usually stayed in the deepest part of the hold and would be the first to be aware if a ship was taking on water. If rats were seen boarding a ship, however, it was a sign that she would enjoy safe passage.

REDHEAD

Red-headed people were believed to be unlucky for a ship. If a sailor met one before boarding, the only way to prevent bad luck was if the sailor spoke first. The colour red is traditionally associated with anger and the devil (though the first depiction of him in Christian iconography is as a blue angel). Judas Iscariot began to be depicted as a redhead in the medieval period when the term "Judas-colour" was used to describe redheads. Paintings often depicted Judas with red hair as a way of marking him out; Shakespeare refers to it in *As You Like It*: "His very hair is of the dissembling colour, something browner than Judas." Later, during the Renaissance, Jewish people were often depicted as having red hair as a negative characteristic.

RED RIBBON

Some shipbuilders, particularly in Scotland, used to attach a red ribbon to the first nail driven into the keel for good luck.[45]

Red Sky

The old phrase "Red sky at night, sailor's delight; red sky in the morning, sailors take warning" likely comes from the Gospel of Matthew 16:2–3: "When evening comes, you say, 'It will be fair weather, for the sky is red,' and in the morning, 'Today it will be stormy, for the sky is red and overcast.'"

Since prevailing winds in the mid-latitudes are westerly, the sailor is able to look to the horizon to see what weather to expect. Red clouds in the morning indicate that the sun is illuminating the underside of rain clouds. In the evening, it means that the sun is in clear enough skies that it can shine on the same rain clouds that will, usually, blow through by the next day. Of course, if a ship is sailing that night then it might not be a sailor's delight. Another rhyme that almost always proves to be true is:

> *When the rain comes before the wind*
> *It's time to get your topsails in*
> *When the wind comes before the rain*
> *You can let them out again*

Other weather-predicting sayings include:

Rainbow to windward—foul falls the day
Rainbow to leeward—damp runs away

Related to the rainbow phenomenon is weather prediction by "sun dogs," a natural phenomenon that occurs when ice crystals are illuminated in the sky, causing "halos" to be seen near the sun:

Dog in the morning, sailors take warning
Dog near to night is a sailor's delight

Cirrus clouds indicate wind and so:

Mares' tails and mackerel scales
Make lofty ships shorten sail

Sailors are always watching for wind shifts for obvious reasons. A drastic shift in wind direction may mean a storm is coming:

When the wind shifts against the sun
Trust it not for back it'll run
When the wind follows the sun
Fine weather will never be done

Predicting the weather by watching the barometer—or "glass"—is a necessary part of watch-keeping duties, and when there is a dramatic change in the barometric measurement then:

Long foretold, long last
Short notice, soon past

First rise, after low
Make all fast, it soon will blow

At sea with low and sinking glass
Soundly sleeps the stupid ass

Only when it's high and rising
Safely sleeps the careful wise one

REMORA

Remora fish were thought to fasten their tails to rocks and then to clamp their jaws to a ship's keel to stop or slow her progress.

Rescuing

For centuries it was considered bad luck to rescue someone who had fallen overboard or who was drowning. "What the sea wants, the sea will have," was a fatalistic belief, coupled with the notion that the sea would also take the rescuer. There was an additional, related belief that rescuing someone would turn him into your enemy: "Save a stranger from the sea, he shall be thy enemy."

Right Foot

Always step onto a boat with your right foot. Leading with the left foot brings bad luck to the voyage. This may stem from the idea that the left side of the body was associated with the devil. The only way to undo the bad luck is to retrace one's steps and then start again, right foot forward. There are others who insist that if you have boarded with your left foot, then you must turn around clockwise three times.

Rings

See also Cramp Rings.

Rings made from the nails or screws of a coffin were thought to protect the wearer from drowning.

Rooster

It is bad luck to hear a rooster crow aboard a ship. This superstition most likely derives from Peter's denial of Christ in Matthew 26:31–35: "'I tell you the truth,' Jesus answered, 'this very night, before the rooster crows, you will disown me three times.'" The rooster was a symbol of Christ because he announces the dawn following the night.

Rope Circle

If a boat is thought to be cursed or jinxed, then a large bight is made in a rope that is then passed over the bow and drawn right around the vessel to the stern. Once the boat has passed through the circle, the curse will have been lifted.

Rowan Tree

Among the Celtic peoples, rowan wood was considered desirable in boat building because it held magical properties. Rowan is also known as mountain ash.

Runes

Norse sailors would carve runes, or sacred verses, into their oars and the bow, stern and rudder of their vessels to appease the gods of wind and sea.[46]

S

SALMON

In Scotland, calling "salmon" by its name was taboo
and meant that none would be caught. It would
sometimes be called the "red fish," or simply the "fish."

SALT

It is bad luck for the salt shaker to be passed directly
to someone else, encapsulated in the phrase "pass salt,
pass sorrow." Spilling salt is also considered unlucky
and to undo this a pinch of the spilled salt must
immediately be cast over the left shoulder. There are
two reasons behind this superstition: the first is that
salt used to be expensive and only the devil would
cause someone to do something so foolish as to spill
salt and, as the devil is always waiting behind the left
shoulder to step in to lead one astray, the pinch of salt
is thrown to blind him. The second reason derives
from Leonardo da Vinci's painting *The Last Supper*,
which depicts Judas Iscariot having knocked the salt
over with his elbow. This incident of spilling salt
created an association between a clumsy person and
bad behaviour, which must have been caused by the
devil, who is, as always, waiting over the left shoulder
to cause more trouble.

Sailors and fishermen have long thought that it is good luck to carry a bit of salt in their pockets. Pomeranian sailors used to throw salt into the sea at the start of a voyage for good luck, while in Scotland, fishermen's wives would throw a handful of salt at their spouses as they set sail. Additionally, the word "salt" was considered unlucky aboard Scottish ships.

Fishermen sometimes carry a pocketful of salt so that if a witch comes aboard to do harm, they can thrust out a handful in the belief that the witch will have to count every grain before casting spells.

Salting In

Nets were "salted in" at the beginning of the season to bring good luck by sprinkling salt all over them.

Salutes

Gun salutes are fired in odd numbers because even numbers are considered unlucky. Odd numbers are considered stronger since they are not readily divisible.

Saluting the Quarterdeck

This tradition dates to ancient Roman seafarers.
Images of the gods were displayed on the quarterdeck,
and everyone stepping aboard had to show their
respect. With the advent of Christianity, a statue
of the Virgin Mary was mounted on the poop deck,
or after deck, which the crew would bow to when
stepping aboard. (The "poop" in poop deck derives
from the Latin word for "doll," used to describe this
small statue.)[47]

Scratching the Mast

See also Backstay.

When becalmed, sailors would sometimes scratch the
mast from the side they wished to see the wind blow.

Seabirds

Seabirds were thought to carry the souls of dead
sailors, and it is considered bad luck to kill them,
particularly the albatross. However, it is considered
good luck if you see one. In Scandinavia, cormorants
are considered a good omen, and in Norway,
cormorants house the spirits of friends lost at sea.

Storm petrels are also known as Mother Carey's chickens, which comes from "Mater Cara," a reference to the Mother of God. In France, they are called "les oiseaux de Notre-Dame" (the birds of Our Lady), sent to protect sailors and warn them of coming storms. The expression "kissed by Mother Carey" means that a child is born to be a sailor and to the sea life, as they were kissed by Mother Carey at birth.

SEA CHEST

A sailor heading to sea will place the key in the lock of their sea chest (the trunk containing their clothes) but not turn it to lock it until they are out of their home. Similarly, once a sailor has packed their bag ashore, nothing will be taken out of it until they are aboard.

SEAHORSE

The seahorse has been considered a lucky charm for sailors ever since the ancient Greeks, who believed that they were a manifestation of Poseidon. Seahorses are believed to protect the souls of drowned sailors until they reach Fiddler's Green.

Seas All

In the early 1900s, a fisherman casting the last net would cry out, "Seas all," rather than "Last net," for the latter would risk the nets being lost.

Sedna

For the Inuit, Sedna is the goddess of the sea and of marine animals, also known as the Mother of the Sea or Mistress of the Sea. She has power over all the sea animals and decides if the Inuit are allowed to harvest them for their own use. If the hunting is bad, then an Inuk shaman would transform himself into a fish and swim down to appease her. One way he does this is to comb and braid her hair, something that she cannot do herself as she has no fingers. Another way to keep her happy is to show respect for any animal killed, which includes giving a drink of fresh water to any seals taken.

SELKIES

In Scotland, selkies—meaning "seal folk"—are
creatures that can change from seals into humans
by shedding their skin. If a selkie is shot while in
its seal guise, a storm will rise when its blood mixes
with the sea.

SEWING

It is bad luck to do any sewing during foul weather
as the bad weather will be sewn into place, and,
conversely, it is good luck to sew in good weather for
the same reason. The same stitch must be used in
every seam to avoid the stitches becoming jealous of
one another and pulling themselves apart.

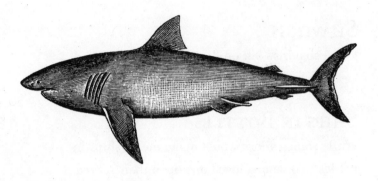

SHARK

A shark following the ship was a sign of the death
of one of the crew. This was based on the belief that
sharks could smell not only blood, but also death. It
was once common practice to catch a shark and then
nail its fin to the end of the jib-boom, not as a good
luck talisman but as a warning to other sharks should
they follow the ship.[48] A separate superstition was that
the shark's fin would bring fair winds.

Shavings

Wood shavings left on deck bring bad luck.[49]

Ships in Bottles

While some sailors would make model ships in
bottles to give to a loved one upon their return or
to sell ashore, most sailors felt that they were a bad
luck talisman to have aboard. They were considered
good luck ashore, however, since the ship depicetd
contained in the bottle would always be safe.

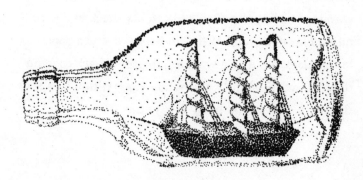

SHIPBUILDING

A person who builds a ship will never sail on her maiden voyage, as it would be unlucky for the vessel in the long run.[50] In Scotland, a crooked or bent coin, traditionally a sixpence, was set in her keel to stop any jealousy between the woods used in construction. Even with this talisman, no shipbuilder would use both juniper and rowan wood in the same boat's construction, as these woods detest one another.

In Vietnam, women were not allowed to climb around or sit on boats that were under construction or the boat would be cursed. Vietnamese shipbuilders also laid a Vietnamese flag along the keel as they began to build the vessel for good luck, and they painted eyes on the bow of the boat to protect her from evil spirits.

Shoes

In England and Scotland, it was once the custom to throw old shoes in the wake of a departing vessel for good luck or for those aboard to throw a pair of old shoes overboard at the start of a long voyage for good luck.[51] However, wearing new shoes on the bridge was unlucky. The practice on some ships was to throw an old pair of shoes overboard in order to bring up the wind, literally "putting the boots to her."

SHROUDS

Never climb between shrouds, but always pass around them on the inboard or outboard side, or you are asking for bad luck. Shrouds are the ropes or wires that support a vessel's mast; they run athwartships at right angles to the keel.

SIRENS

Sirens are half woman and half bird who lure sailors, through their irresistible singing, into dangerous waters where they will be shipwrecked. This is the etymology of the word "siren," meaning an alarm.

Snakes

In India, sailors would keep live venomous snakes aboard. If the snakes were lethargic, then it was an omen of bad weather and the boats would not put to sea, but if the snakes were lively and active, then it predicted good weather.[52]

Sneezing

Sneezing to the right at the start of a voyage is good luck; sneezing to the left is a bad omen.

Socks

See also Mittens.

Grey socks are considered to be a "Jonah." One
superstition in New England was to knit hair into
the toes of sailors' socks to ensure their wearer's
safe return.

South Bay Bessie

Very similar to the Loch Ness Monster in Scotland,
the Ogopogo in Okanagan Lake, the Cadborosaurus
of Vancouver Island and numerous others around
the world, South Bay Bessie, in Lake Erie, was first
sighted in 1793; it is a twelve-metre-long snake-like
beast with a dog-shaped head, sparkling eyes and a
pointed tail.

Sou'wester

A yellow Sou'wester is frowned upon as being bad luck since it is perceived to resemble a banana. A Sou'wester is a traditional rain hat with a long brim at the back to protect the wearer's neck.

Speaking

Speaking to a boat to encourage her along greatly increases her speed. Sailors would not consider this as superstitious, although others might.

Spiders

It is considered bad luck to kill spiders on board because they embody the spirits of ancient mariners: "If you wish to thrive—let the spider stay alive." On ships from Iceland, if a spider on a ship is seen climbing up its web, then fair weather will follow, while the reverse is true if the spider is climbing downward. Breaking a spider's web aboard was also considered unlucky.

Spitting

Spitting into a vessel's hold is bad luck.[53]

Starboard Side

Since the 1880s, and perhaps until today, Irish fishermen always board on the starboard side of their vessel no matter the inconvenience that this might cause.

Stars

It is bad luck to try to count all the stars in the sky, because once the one hundredth is reached, it traditionally means death.

Steering

The sailor at the helm must
have clean hands.

Stirring

Stirring one's tea (or anything else in a cup or mug)
with a knife invites bad luck: "Stir with a knife and
stir up strife."

Stolen

In Pomerania, a stolen piece of wood put into the keel
while she is being built will make a ship sail faster.[54]
A common belief in fishing is that stolen tackle or
lures will increase your chance of catching fish.

Stone

In the Hebrides there is an upright stone on Iona Island that gives the power of being able to steer a ship well to anyone that stretches their arm along it.

Stones

Throwing stones into the ocean causes storms with large ocean swells. A stone thrown over a vessel that is putting out to sea ensures she will never return. A white stone found in the ballast means bad luck.[55]

Sulphur

Smelling sulphur while at sea is bad luck as it means Satan has constructed a ship from it, which he uses to collect drowned sailors.

Sun

When given the choice, always turn the vessel clockwise, or deosil—that is, keeping to the right of the sun. Turning counter-clockwise, known as turning widdershins, brings bad luck.

Swallows and Curlews

Swallows seen at sea are a good sign, while curlews are bad luck. Swallows can fly long distances and then return home safely. On the Great Lakes, some sailors mark every 5,000 nautical miles sailed with a tattoo of a swallow. In ancient Greece, swallows were associated with the goddess of love, Aphrodite, who typically brought good fortune and happiness. Sighting a swallow when homeward bound was a good omen, because it meant that land was near and the voyage would soon be over.

Swearing

Swearing aboard is an insult to Neptune, who will bring stormy weather in return. Navy ships were once governed by the *Black Book of the Admiralty*, which followed the Laws of Oléron. The penalty for swearing at, insulting or vilifying another member of the crew aboard was to pay him "as many ounces of silver as times he has reviled him." The penalty for committing murder was that the murderer be tied to the corpse and thrown overboard.[56]

Sweeping

Sweeping the deck after dark means someone will drown.[57]

T

Tailor / Dressmaker

To meet a tailor or dressmaker while heading to
the vessel means bad luck for the voyage. These
professions must also never be mentioned in the
presence of someone preparing for a voyage, for the
same reason.

Tattoos

A widespread preconception is that tattoos were popular
among seafarers because they functioned as a form of
identification if they drowned, and their bodies were
recovered. However, the purpose of some common
images inked onto sailors was either to encourage good
luck or to ward off bad luck. The anchor was thought
to keep a sailor who had fallen overboard from straying
from the ship, given the anchor is always attached to
the vessel. A nautical star or a compass rose placed on
the web between the thumb and forefinger would help
to guide a sailor safely back home.

Despite the superstition against having a pig
aboard, having one tattooed on the foot or leg, with a
hen tattooed on the opposite limb, protected against
drowning. This may have derived from the practice
of keeping these animals in wooden crates, which if

in a shipwreck, would usually be found still afloat, the animals still alive: "Pig on the knee—safety at sea." A more religious explanation is that pigs and chickens are both land animals, and if God were to see them in the ocean, he would take pity on them and remove them to shore. These tattoos, in combination, are commonly known as "ham and eggs" and ensure that their bearer will never go hungry.

Another common tattoo was to have the words HOLD and FAST tattooed across the knuckles, to help keep a sailor from losing their grip aloft and falling to the deck. The phrase "hold fast" most likely has a Christian basis, as it appears six times in the Bible, the first citation being in Deuteronomy 10:20: "Fear the Lord your God and serve him. Hold fast to him and take your oaths in his name." A crucifix or a portrait of Jesus was sometimes tattooed across a sailor's back, perhaps to show his devotion to God, but also so that if he were to be flogged for breaking the rules the bosun swinging the cat-o-nine-tails might be more inclined to show mercy, perhaps to protect his own soul as he might then be called to answer to a higher power for disrespecting a holy image.

The superstitions of nautical tattoos should not be confused with the meaning of them as associated in particular with United States Navy. For instance in the USN an anchor tattoo symbolizes that its wearer has crossed the Atlantic and a hula girl or palm tree means that the sailor has been to Hawaii.

THIRD VESSEL

"To be the third vessel in line leaving harbour is still unlucky and ingenious Ulstermen may still lash leading boats together and pass through them as one, to confound malignant spirits."[58]

THIRTEEN

The number thirteen is often considered unlucky aboard. One belief is that there were thirteen people at the Last Supper, with Judas Iscariot being the last—and, therefore, the thirteenth person—to arrive. In Norse mythology, one legend is that at a feast held for only twelve of the gods, an uninvited thirteenth god arrived, Loki, who was the god of mischief and disorder and subsequently caused the death of another of the gods.

Thread

Winding thread onto a spool after sunset was believed
to throw a loved one's vessel off course. In the early
1900s in England, there was an additional belief that
if a wife did so, it portended that she would soon be
sewing her husband's burial shroud.

Toasting

Never toast with water, because doing so brings
bad luck.

Touch Wood

The widespread practice of touching wood, or
knocking on wood, dates to pagan times and may
be found in many cultures around the world. The
tradition derives from the belief that trees contained
spirits that would help the person who awakened them
with their knock. At sea, when a sailor predicted
the occurrence of a good event or good fortune, they
would ensure they touched or knocked on wood.

Towing

If a vessel is being towed out to sea and develops a slight list to port, she will have a lucky passage, while a list to starboard means an unlucky one.

Traveller's Tree

A piece of wood from a traveller's tree was often carried by sailors as a good luck charm to prevent his ship from becoming lost. A traveller's tree is a plant from Madagascar resembling a palm tree.

Turf

In Iceland, a sailor would cut a small piece of turf from a graveyard and carry it with him to prevent seasickness.

TURTLES

If a turtle is killed but not eaten, it will bring bad luck to the ship. Sailors who carry turtle bones in their pockets enjoy good luck.

U

UMBRELLAS

Umbrellas are for use in foul weather ashore, as they are impractical on a ship; bringing one on board is thought to tempt fate and to bring on a storm.

UNLUCKY SHIP

If a ship was deemed unlucky, either by suffering one accident too many aboard or, in the case of a fishing vessel, not catching enough fish, she was given a big bump, when coming back into harbour, hitting the dock or a shoal to knock the evil spirits and witches out of her. Another method was to carry torches all around the decks to burn away any bad spirits. Bad luck boats are referred to as "hoodoo ships."

Walking Sticks

Walking sticks, or canes, were
considered lucky because they
resembled magicians' wands,
and they were often collected or
carved by sailors.

Walnut Wood

Walnut wood is considered
to bring bad luck and was
consequently avoided in the
construction of ships. In North America this
superstition derives from the belief that walnut trees
attract lightning. The same superstition existed
in Europe, although it was based on the belief that
walnut trees were considered bewitched, because no
other plant or tree thrived near them.

Waterspouts

Arab mariners in the medieval period considered waterspouts to be dragons that they called *tannin*. The Japanese had a similar belief and called them *tatsumaki*. The Chinese also conceived of them as dragons and believed that they were attempting to drag good sailors up into the heavens. European sailors commonly reacted to them by firing the ship's guns into them or slashing at them with a black-handled knife while reciting the Gospel of John, something that Christopher Columbus is said to have done.

WAVES

As waves build to become larger and larger, it is believed that the ninth wave will always be the most destructive.

WEBBED FEET

People with webbed feet never drown.

WEDDING RING

The tradition of wearing a wedding ring on the third finger of the left hand originated with the notion that an artery runs from this finger to the heart. The ring has not always been worn on this finger, and among sailors, it was typically worn on the index finger.[59]

WHALE'S BREATH

It is good luck to be "breathed" upon by a whale when it spouts.

WHEEL

The wheel or helm of a motor vessel is often set on the starboard side—the right-hand side of God.

Whistling

The prohibition against whistling aboard is thought to date back to Viking explorers, when they would whistle to Thor, god of thunder, who would whistle in return, causing the wind to blow a gale. Whistling is thought to challenge the wind to blow in return. On some ships, the youngest crew member is granted permission from the captain to whistle when the vessel is becalmed, as it is believed that Thor would not feel threatened by someone young.

In another context, whistling was forbidden aboard Royal Navy ships because, on occasion, it had been used as a code among mutineers to signal each other and coordinate their actions. There was also the practical consideration that orders were communicated by the bosun's whistle; therefore, another sailor whistling might inadvertently interfere with this system and cause confusion among the crew. This is the same reason that whistling is not allowed backstage in theatres except as a direction for changing scenery or curtains.

The ship's cook was given leeway to whistle and, indeed, was encouraged to do so aboard Royal Navy

vessels. It proved to
the crew that he wasn't
helping himself to their
rations, as it is quite
difficult to whistle with
one's mouth full.

WIND

Acknowledging the
wind when it is fair
will cause it to change
direction.

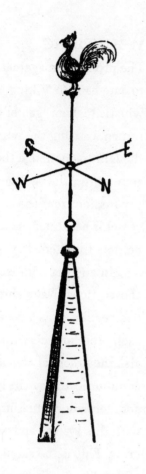

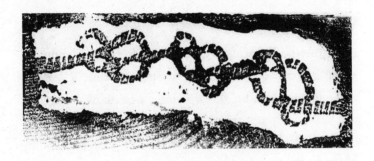

Wind Knots

See also Bags of Wind.

Wind knots were popular purchases from women
perceived to be witches for those heading out on a
long voyage. Three knots were tied by the witch
or sorceress in a piece of rope or cloth. When the
sailor later needed the wind to blow, he would untie
the first knot, which would cause a gentle breeze to
come. Untying the second knot would bring a gale,
and untying the third knot released a hurricane. The
act of buying the wind knots was known as "raising
the wind."

Windog

A segment of a rainbow's arc is a sign that a strong wind is coming.[60] It is very similar to a sundog but only appears as a bright orb along a rainbow's arc.

Windshield Wipers

Windshield wipers aboard are often set to port for good luck.

Wine

Pouring wine on the deck as an offering to the gods will bring good luck on a long voyage.

Women

Women were considered bad luck at sea since they might distract the male sailors from their duties, which would be an opportunity for the sea to wreak havoc. There is also the belief that the sea is a feminine being and she will be jealous of any attention directed toward women aboard rather than to her.

Words

Many unlucky words and phrases have already been covered, but the list includes "drowned," "goodbye," "good luck," "pig," "fox," "cat," "dog," "rabbit" and anything to do with the church. The only way to reverse the bad luck was to draw blood, usually by punching the speaker in the nose. Furthermore, Scottish fishermen never say "minister," "kirk," "salmon," "swine" or "dog."

Wren

The feather of a wren killed on New Year's Day protects sailors from drowning in a shipwreck. This belief comes from the old story of a mermaid who lured sailors into the depths to drown. However, a knight found that the feather of a wren would protect against her spell. She, in turn, would transform into a wren each New Year's Day; therefore, a feather from a wren killed on that day would offer magical protection for whoever possessed it, as she would then fly back ashore and leave the sailors aboard in peace. Manx sailors sailed with a dead wren aboard, because while as an evil spirit it would bring storms, it would eventually turn itself into a wren and fly away, leaving calm seas.

Endnotes

1   Chris Hillier, *The Devil and the Deep: A Guide to Nautical Myths and Superstitions* (London: Adlard Coles Nautical, 1997), 10.

2   Homer, *The Odyssey* (Boston, New York: Houghton Mifflin & Co., 1892), 147.

3   Hillier, *The Devil and the Deep*, 15.

4   Michael Brown, ed., *The Hamish Hamilton Book of Sea Legends* (London: Hamish Hamilton Children's Books, 1971), 172.

5   Brown, *Book of Sea Legends*, 72.

6   Brown, 173.

7   W.N.T. Beckett, *A Few Naval Customs, Expressions, Traditions and Superstitions* (Portsmouth, UK: Gieves Ltd., 1930), 26.

8   Angelo Rappoport, *Superstitions of Sailors* (London: Stanley Paul & Co., 1928), 41.

9   Helen Creighton, *Bluenose Magic: Popular Beliefs and Superstitions in Nova Scotia* (Toronto: Ryerson Press, 1968), 121.

10   Creighton, *Bluenose Magic*, 121.

11 Peter D. Jeans, *Seafaring Lore & Legend: A Miscellany of Maritime Myth, Superstition, Fable, and Fact* (Camden, ME: International Marine, 2007), 318.

12 Hillier, *The Devil and the Deep*, 28.

13 Hillier, *The Devil and the Deep*, 29.

14 Fletcher S. Bassett, *Legends and Superstitions of the Sea and Sailors* (Detroit: Singing Tree Press, 1971), 429.

15 Hillier, *The Devil and the Deep*, 33.

16 Jeans, *Seafaring Lore & Legend*, 305.

17 Vernon Oickle, *Red Sky at Night: Superstitions and Wives' Tales Compiled by Atlantic Canada's Most Eclectic Collector* (Lunenburg, NS: MacIntyre Purcell Publishing Inc, 2011), 157.

18 Angelo S. Rappoport, *Superstitions of Sailors* (London: Stanley Paul & Co., 1928), 77.

19 Bassett, *Legends and Superstitions*, 108.

20 Bassett, 140.

21 Bassett, 140.

22 Hillier, *The Devil and the Deep*, 71.

23 Hillier, 38.

24 Bassett, *Legends and Superstitions*, 470.

25 Gerard Carruthers, ed., *Burns: Poems by Robert Burns* (Toronto: Random House, 2006), 62.

26 Aristotle, cited in Rappoport, *Superstitions of Sailors*, 42.

27 Creighton, *Bluenose Magic*, 127.

28 Margaret Baker, *The Folklore of the Sea* (Newton Abbot, UK; North Pomfret, VT: David & Charles, 1979), 15.

29 Bassett, *Legends and Superstitions*, 469.

30 Horace Beck, *Folklore and the Sea* (Edison, NJ: Castle Books, 1973), 309.

31 Hillier, *The Devil and the Deep*, 50.

32 Bassett, *Legends and Superstitions*, 427.

33 Bassett, 276.

34 Brown, *Book of Sea Legends*, 78.

35 Brown, 159.

36 Creighton, *Bluenose Magic*, 123.

37 Creighton, 120.

38 Hillier, *The Devil and the Deep*, 69.

39 D. Arnold-Forster, *The Ways of the Navy* (London: Ward, Lock & Co., 1931), 117.

40 Bassett, *Legends and Superstitions*, 431.

41 Creighton, *Bluenose Magic*, 122.

42 Hillier, *The Devil and the Deep*, 85.

43 Jeans, *Seafaring Lore & Legend*, 310.

44 Jeans, 292.

45 Hillier, *The Devil and the Deep*, 73.

46 Bassett, *Legends and Superstitions*, 139.

47 Stan Hugill, *Songs of the Sea: The Tales and Tunes of Sailors and Sailing Ships* (Maidenhead, UK: McGraw-Hill, 1977), 180.

48 Jeans, *Seafaring Lore & Legend*, 314.

49 Creighton, *Bluenose Magic*, 97.

50 Creighton, 119.

51 Bassett, *Legends and Superstitions*, 108.

52 Bassett, 241.

53 Creighton, *Bluenose Magic*, 123.

54 Bassett, *Legends and Superstitions*, 433.

55 Creighton, *Bluenose Magic*, 126.

56 Beckett, *A Few Naval Customs, Expressions, Traditions and Superstitions*, 3.

57 Creighton, *Bluenose Magic*, 97.

58 Baker, *The Folklore of the Sea*, 90.

59 Edward Smedley et al., *The Occult Sciences: Sketches of the Traditions and Superstitions of Past Times, and the Marvels of the Present Day* (London, Glasgow: Richard Griffin and Co., 1855), 361.

60 Beckett, *A Few Naval Customs, Expressions, Traditions and Superstitions*, 47.

References

Archibald, Malcolm. *Sixpence for the Wind: A Knot of Nautical Folklore*. Toronto: Dundurn Publishing, 1998.

Arnold-Forster, D. *The Ways of the Navy*. London: Ward, Lock & Co., 1931.

Baker, Margaret. *The Folklore of the Sea*. Newton Abbot, UK; North Pomfret, VT: David & Charles, 1979.

Bassett, Fletcher S. *Legends and Superstitions of the Sea and Sailors*. Detroit: Singing Tree Press, 1971.

Beck, Horace. *Folklore and the Sea*. Edison, NJ: Castle Books, 1973.

Beckett, W.N.T. *A Few Naval Customs, Expressions, Traditions and Superstitions*. Portsmouth, UK: Gieves Ltd., 1930.

Brown, Michael, ed. *The Hamish Hamilton Book of Sea Legends*. London: Hamish Hamilton Children's Books Ltd., 1971.

Carruthers, Gerard, ed. *Burns: Poems by Robert Burns*. Toronto: Random House, 2006.

Cielo, Astra. *Signs, Omens and Superstitions*. New York: George Sully & Co., 1918.

Coleridge, Samuel Taylor. *The Rime of the Ancyent Marinere*. New York: Reynal and Hitchcock, 1946.

Creighton, Helen. *Bluenose Magic: Popular Beliefs and Superstitions in Nova Scotia*. Toronto: Ryerson Press, 1968.

Hillier, Chris. *The Devil and the Deep: A Guide to Nautical Myths and Superstitions*. London: Adlard Coles Nautical, 1997.

Homer. *The Odyssey*. Translated by George Herbert Palmer. New York, Boston: Houghton, Mifflin & Co., 1892.

Hugill, Stan. *Songs of the Sea: The Tales and Tunes of Sailors and Sailing Ships*. Maidenhead, UK: McGraw-Hill, 1977.

Jeans, Peter D. *Seafaring Lore & Legend: A Miscellany of Maritime Myth, Superstition, Fable, and Fact*. Camden, ME: International Marine, 2007.

Jones, William. *Finger-Ring Lore: Historical, Legendary, Anecdotal*. London: Chatto and Windus, 1877.

Lamont-Brown, Raymond. *Phantoms of the Sea: Legends, Customs, and Superstitions*. New York: Taplinger Publishing Company, 1972.

Oickle, Vernon. *Red Sky at Night: Superstitions and Wives' Tales Compiled by Atlantic Canada's most Eclectic Collector*. Lunenburg, NS: MacIntyre Purcell Publishing Inc., 2011.

Pliny the Elder. *The Natural History of Pliny*. Vol. 5. London: Henry G. Bohn, 1856.

Rappoport, Angelo S. *Superstitions of Sailors*. London: Stanley Paul & Co, 1928.

Smedley, Edward, William C. Taylor, Henry Thompson and Elihu Rich. *The Occult Sciences: Sketches of the Traditions and Superstitions of Past Times, and the Marvels of the Present Day*. London, Glasgow: Richard Griffin and Company, 1855.

Stonehouse, Frederick. *Haunted Lakes: Great Lakes Ghost Stories, Superstitions, and Sea Serpents*. Lake Superior Port Cities, 1997.

R. BRUCE MACDONALD is a writer, sailor and artist
with a passion for Canadian history. Macdonald has
logged over 100,000 nautical miles and, for many
years, lived along the BC coast aboard *North Star* with
his family. He is the author of *North Star of Herschel
Island* (Friesen Press, 2012) and *Sisters of the Ice*
(Lost Moose Books, 2021).